ONE body, ONE Spirit

WORSHIP SONGS FOR A NEW GENERATION

Copyright © 2001 by Pilot Point Music, Box 419527, Kansas City, MO 64141.
All rights reserved. Litho in U.S.A.

Lillenas° PUBLISHING COMPANY
KANSAS CITY, MO 64141

www.lillenas.com

CONTENTS

Let Everything That Has Breath

Words and Music by
MATT REDMAN

PLEASE NOTE: Copying of this product is not covered by CCLI licenses. For CCLI information call 1-800-234-2446.

You Are My Rock

Words and Music by
JOEL AUGE

PLEASE NOTE: Copying of this product is not covered by CCLI licenses. For CCLI information call 1-800-234-2446.

One Body, One Spirit

Words and Music by
CHARLIE HALL

1. Fath-er we come to You ... in spir-it and truth

2. Fath-er I want to keep ... the u-ni-ty___

14

(to pg. 12, meas. 9)

One bod - y, one spir - it, one hope of our___ call.

One faith and one bap - ti - sm, one Fath - er of___ all

18

Hold Me Now

Words and Music by
KENDALL COMBS

CCLI Song #3293359. For CCLI information call 1-800-234-2446.

Hold me now.

(to pg. 22, meas. 9)

D.S.
(to pg. 24, meas. 25)

Hold me now.

D.S.
(to pg. 24, meas. 25)

Hold____ me now.____

Hold____ me now.____

Hold____ me now.____

The Lamb Who Was Slain

SAL OLIVERI

JEFF NELSON

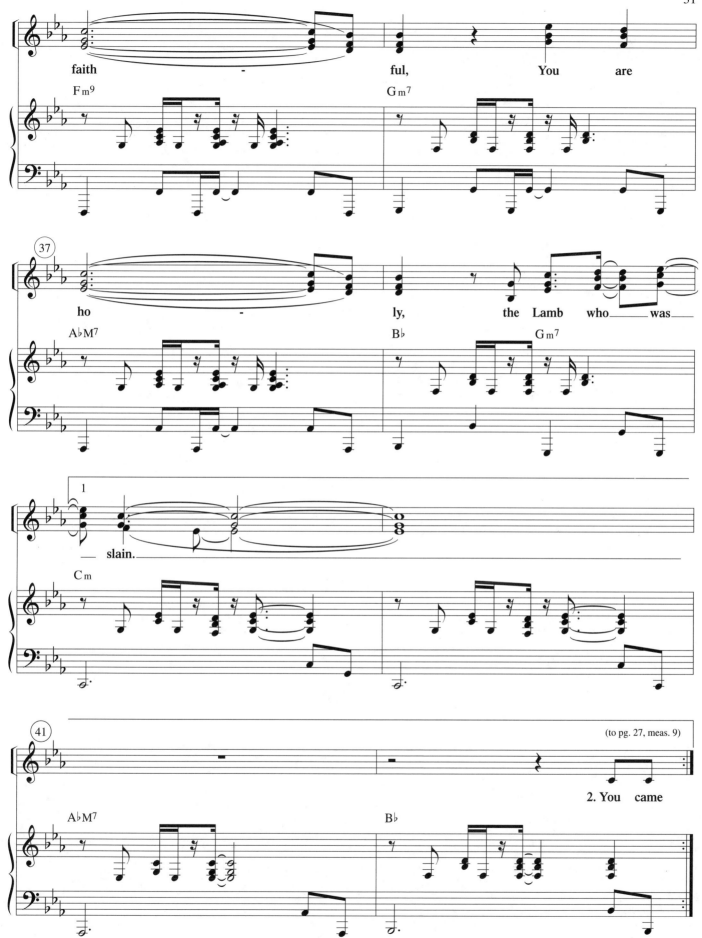

(to pg. 27, meas. 9)

D.S.
(to pg. 29, meas. 25)

See How Mercy

Words and Music by
GARY SCHMIDT

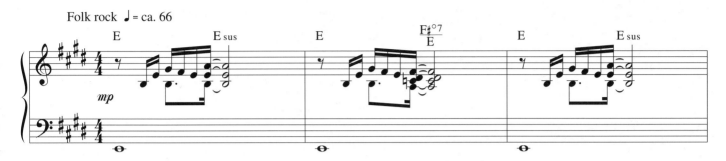

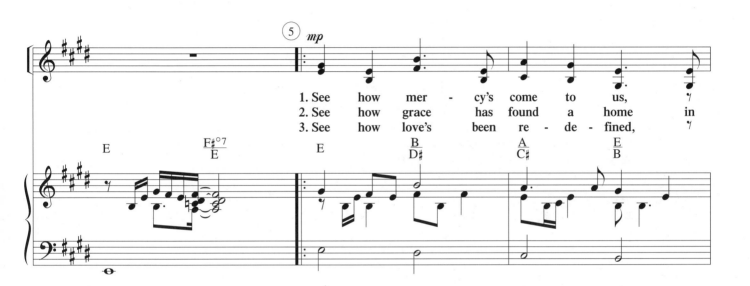

1. See how mer - cy's come to us,
2. See how grace has found a home in
3. See how love's been re - de - fined,

sin - ners who_____ de - serve the cross._____
prod - i - gals_____ who love to roam._____
lives ex - changed,_____ His for mine._____ When

CCLI Song #2976684. **For CCLI information call 1-800-234-2446.**

In our dark - ness and our___ shame,
Such am I and such are___ we, yet
on the cross He took my___ place, no

it's a won - der ℽ that He___
Fa - ther waits___ ex - pect - ant -
doubt my Sav - ior He ℽ saw my___

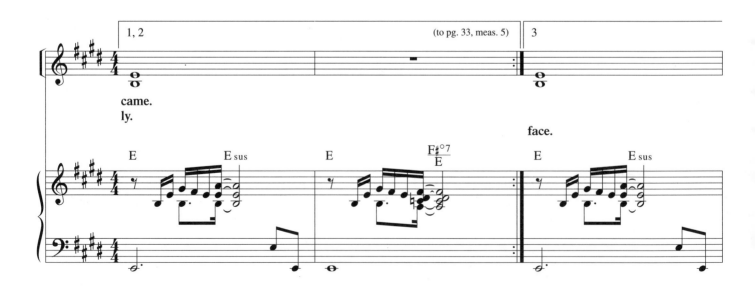

came.
ly.
face.

All of My Life

Words and Music by
CASSIDY HARRIS

1. I have been thro' this before,
2. With these words I come to You, Lord.

CCLI Song #3293373. For CCLI information call 1-800-234-2446.

We Fall Down

Words and Music by
CHRIS TOMLIN

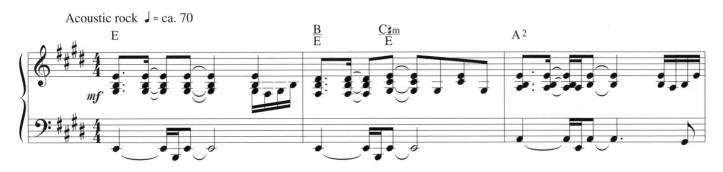

We fall down, we lay our crowns at the feet

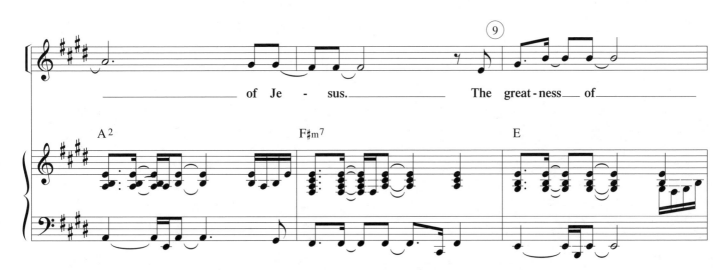

of Je - sus. The great - ness of

PLEASE NOTE: Copying of this product is not covered by CCLI licenses. For CCLI information call 1-800-234-2446.

(to pg. 41, meas. 5)

D.S.
(to pg. 42, meas. 13)

We cry,

We fall down, we lay our crowns at the feet of Je-

-sus. The great-ness of

Glory to You

Words and Music by
JENNIFER MARTIN

48

(to pg. 46, meas. 20)

Psalm 139
(Great Is Your Love)

Words and Music by
CHARLIE HALL

Lord, You've searched ____ me and ____ You know ____ me, when I sit, when I rise. ____

54

Your tho'ts t'ward me,____ O God,____ out -

56

O Sacred King

Words and Music by
MATT REDMAN

58

How can I hon-or You right-ly, hon-or that's fit for Your name? O— sa-cred Friend, O— ho-ly Friend, I don't take what You give light-ly, friend-ship in - stead of dis - grace. For it's the

those who rec - og - nize Your pow'r know

just how won - der - ful You are, that You _____ draw

near.

What a Friend I've Found

Words and Music by
MARTIN SMITH

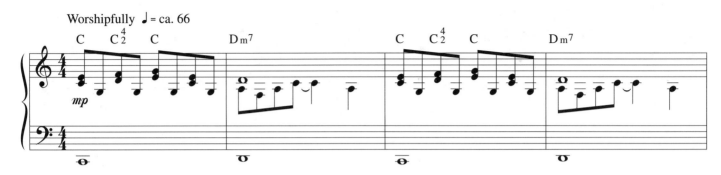

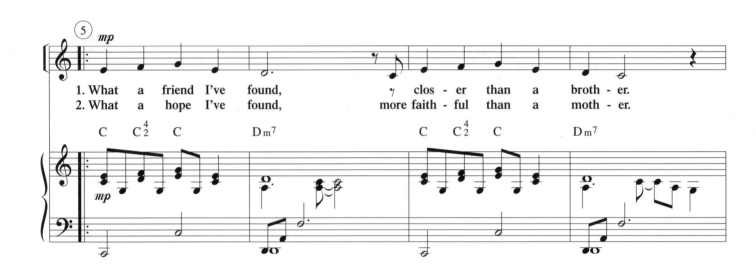

1. What a friend I've found, closer than a broth-er.
2. What a hope I've found, more faith-ful than a moth-er.

I have felt Your touch, more in-ti-mate than lov-ers.
It would break my heart to ev-er lose each oth-er.

PLEASE NOTE: Copying of this product is not covered by CCLI licenses. For CCLI information call 1-800-234-2446.

Let Everything That Has Breath

Words and Music by
MATT REDMAN

PLEASE NOTE: Copying of this product is not covered by CCLI licenses. For CCLI information call 1-800-234-2446.

65

66

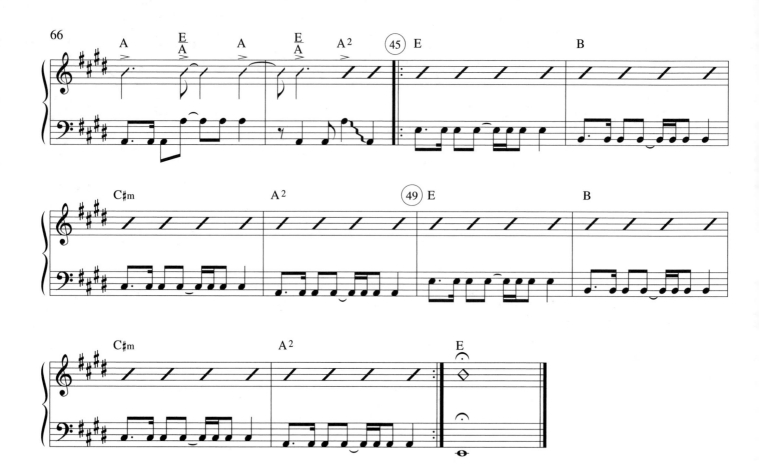

This page is intentionally blank
to minimize page turns.

You Are My Rock

Words and Music by
JOEL AUGE

One Body, One Spirit

Words and Music by
CHARLIE HALL

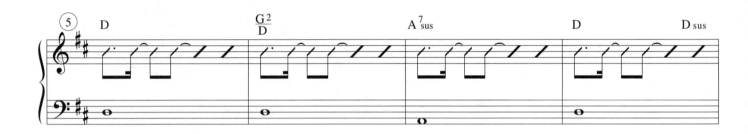

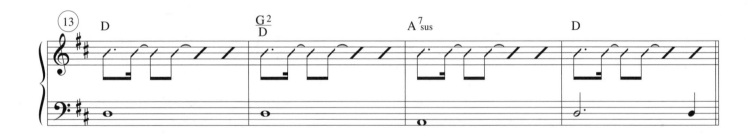

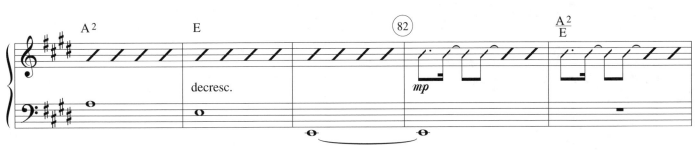

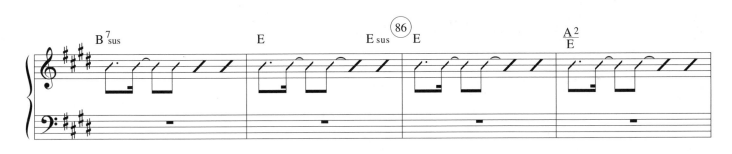

Hold Me Now

Words and Music by
KENDALL COMBS

CCLI Song #3293359. For CCLI information call 1-800-234-2446.

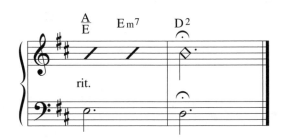

The Lamb Who Was Slain

SAL OLIVERI

JEFF NELSON

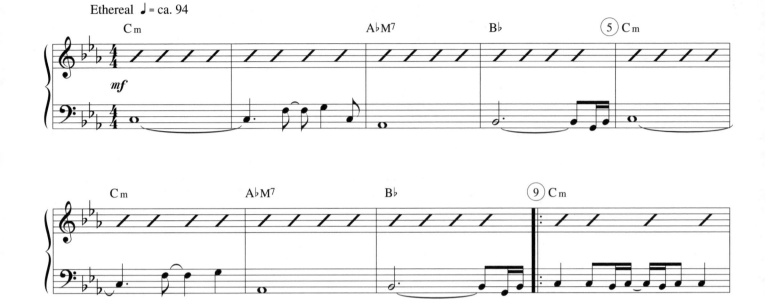

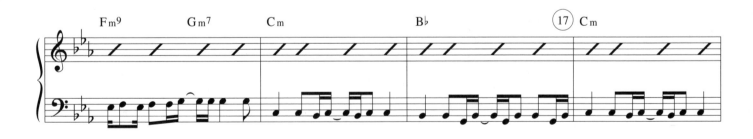

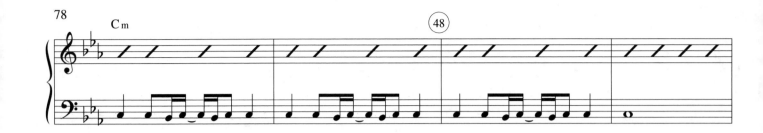

This page is intentionally blank
to minimize page turns.

See How Mercy

Words and Music by
GARY SCHMIDT

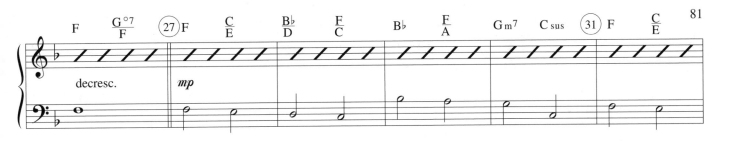

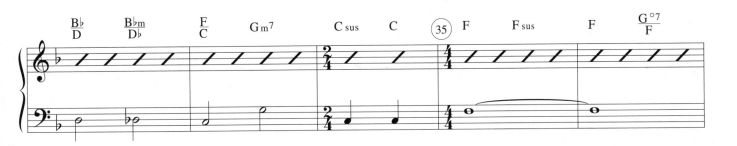

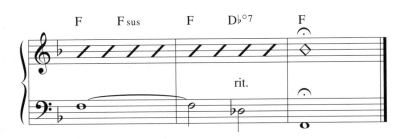

All of My Life

Words and Music by
CASSIDY HARRIS

CCLI Song #3293373. For CCLI information call 1-800-234-2446.

We Fall Down

Words and Music by
CHRIS TOMLIN

Glory to You

Words and Music by
JENNIFER MARTIN

88

(to pg. 87, meas. 20)
(to pg. 87, meas. 20)

Psalm 139
(Great Is Your Love)

Words and Music by
CHARLIE HALL

Gently ♩ = ca. 92

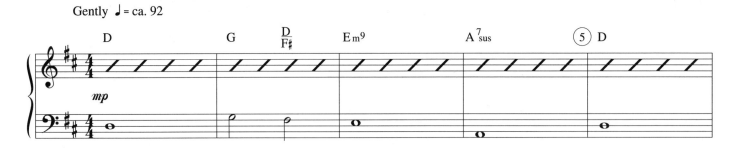

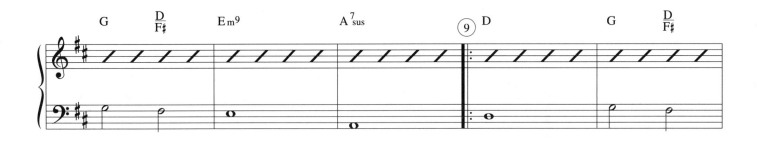

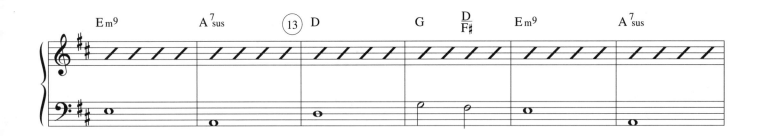

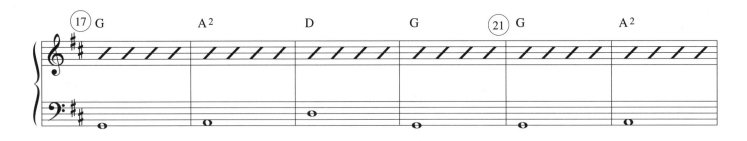

O Sacred King

Words and Music by
MATT REDMAN

This page is intentionally blank
to minimize page turns.

What a Friend I've Found

Words and Music by
MARTIN SMITH

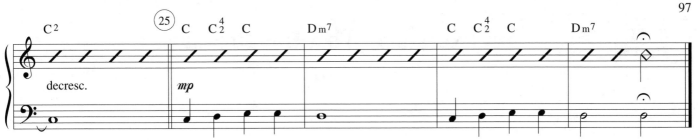

Let Everything That Has Breath

Words and Music by
MATT REDMAN

Let ev - 'ry - thing___ that, ev - 'ry - thing___ that,

ev - 'ry - thing_____ that has___ breath praise the Lord.

Ev - 'ry - thing_____ that, ev - 'ry - thing_____ that,

ev - 'ry - thing_____ that has___ breath praise the Lord.

This page is intentionally blank
to minimize page turns.

You Are My Rock

Words and Music by
JOEL AUGE

One Body, One Spirit

Words and Music by
CHARLIE HALL

1. Fath-er we come to You in spir-it and truth

2. Fath-er I want to keep the u - ni - ty

with our heart and our mind.

of the Spir-it in the bond of peace.

(to pg. 104, meas. 9)

108

Hold Me Now

Words and Music by
KENDALL COMBS

CCLI Song #3293359. For CCLI information call 1-800-234-2446.

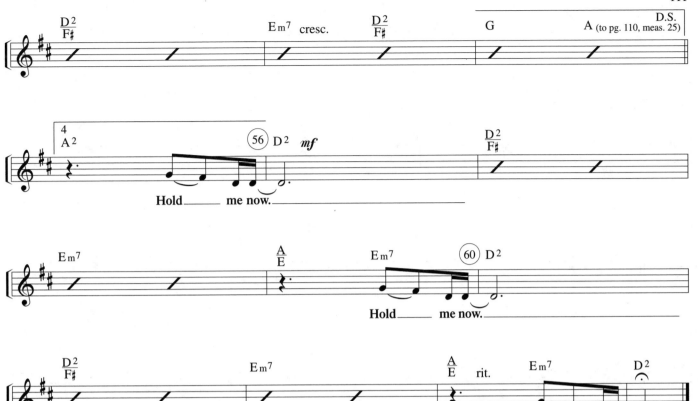

The Lamb Who Was Slain

SAL OLIVERI

JEFF NELSON

Ethereal ♩ = ca. 94

Lyrics:

1. You have o - pened the door of the rich - es of God and poured out Your life for the lost, the Lamb who was slain. You e -

(2. You came) down as a man and you suf - fered the cross. The King of the heav - ens be - came the Lamb who was slain. But our

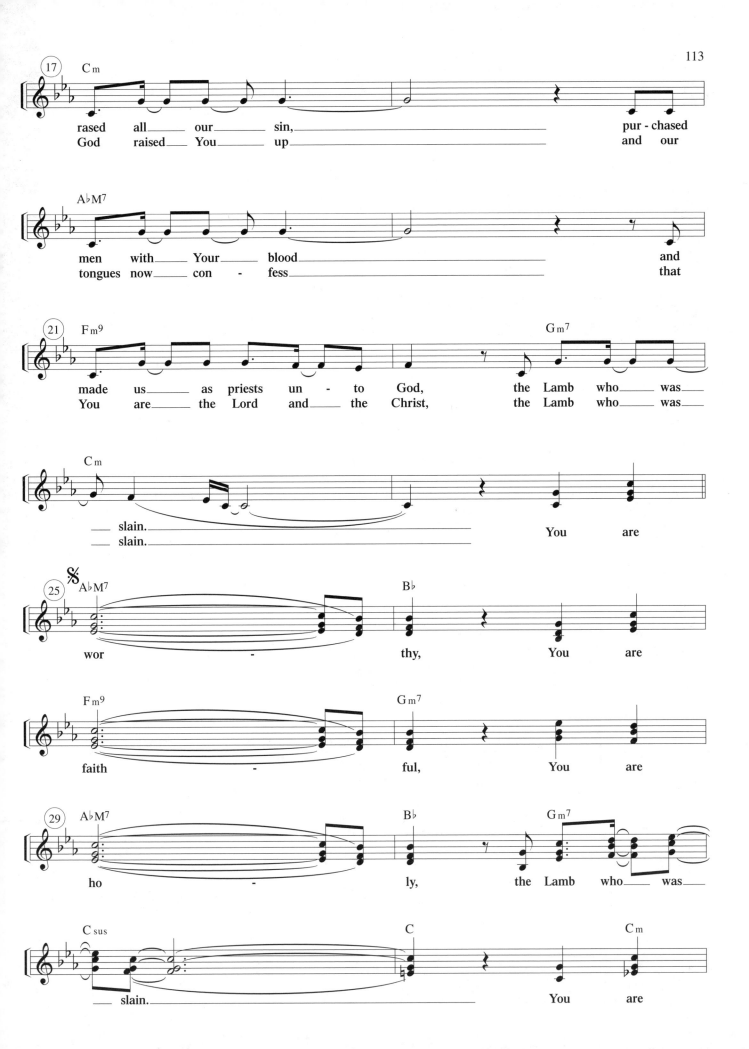

This page is intentionally blank
to minimize page turns.

See How Mercy

Words and Music by
GARY SCHMIDT

CCLI song #2976684. For CCLI information call 1-800-234-2446.

All of My Life

Words and Music by
CASSIDY HARRIS

We Fall Down

Words and Music by
CHRIS TOMLIN

PLEASE NOTE: Copying of this product is not covered by CCLI licenses. For CCLI information call 1-800-234-2446.

We cry

We cry

"Ho — ly, ho — ly, ho — ly   is___ the_ Lamb!"___

Glory to You

Words and Music by
JENNIFER MARTIN

124

(to pg. 123, meas. 20)

You are___

Fath - er and Cre - a - tor___ God,

Mak - er of___ heav - en___ and Mak - er of___ Earth.

We wor - ship___ You, we give You___ thanks.

We praise You!___

You are___ Fath - er and

Cre - a - tor___ God, Mak - er of___ heav - en___ and

Mak - er of___ Earth. We wor - ship___ You,

we give You___ thanks. We praise

(to pg. 123, meas. 20)

Psalm 139
(Great Is Your Love)

Words and Music by
CHARLIE HALL

Lord, You've searched me and You know me, when I sit, when I rise. You un-der-stand my tho'ts and my deeds and I can-not hide from You. Your tho'ts t'ward me, O God, out-num-ber all the sand.

128

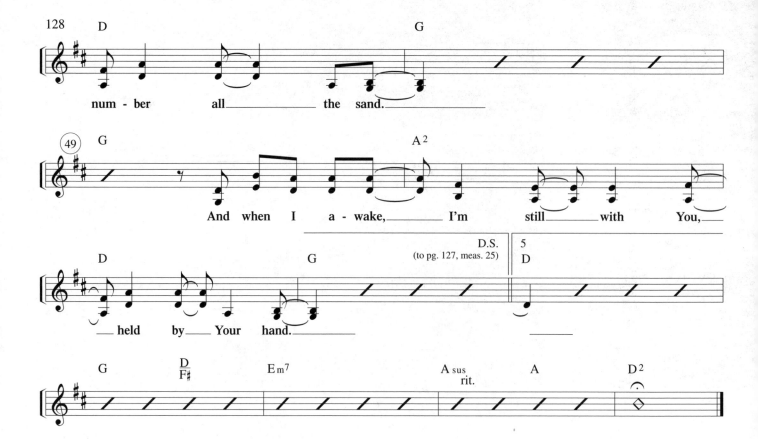

num - ber all the sand.

And when I a - wake, I'm still with You,

held by Your hand.

D.S.
(to pg. 127, meas. 25)

O Sacred King

Words and Music by
MATT REDMAN

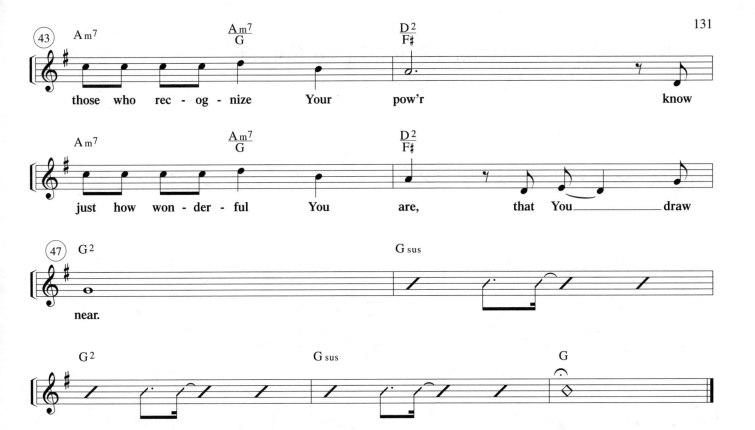

those who rec - og - nize Your pow'r know

just how won - der - ful You are, that You_____draw

near.

What a Friend I've Found

Words and Music by
MARTIN SMITH

1. What a friend I've found, closer than a broth - er.
2. What a hope I've found, more faith - ful than a moth - er.

I have felt Your touch, more in - ti - mate than lov - ers.
It would break my heart to ev - er lose each oth - er.

Je - sus! Je - sus!

Je - sus, friend for - ev - er!

er! er!

What a friend I've found, clos - er than a broth - er.

Let Everything that Has Breath

Chorus
>   Let everything that, everything that,
>   Everything that has breath praise the Lord.
>   Everything that, everything that,
>   Everything that has breath praise the Lord.

1. Praise You in the morning, praise You in the evening,
   Praise You when I'm young and when I'm old.
   Praise You when I'm laughing, praise You when I'm grieving,
   Praise You every season of the soul.

   If we could see how much You're worth, Your power,
      Your might, Your endless love,
   Then surely we would never cease to praise You!

2. Praise You in the heavens, joining with the angels,
   Praising You forever and a day.
   Praise You on the earth, now, joining with creation,
   Calling all the nations to Your praise.

   If they could see how much You're worth, Your power,
      Your might, Your endless love,
   Then surely they would never cease to praise You!

You Are My Rock

Chorus
Lord, let Your rain fall down, 'cause
You are my Rock, You are my Rock.
Wash away the sand and the clay,
'Cause You are my Rock, You are my Rock.

And when I fall and need something stable,
You are my Rock, You are my Rock.
I fall on my knees and lay down at Your table,
'Cause You are my Rock, yeah, You are my Rock.

Bridge
And when I fall You pick me up and bring me there.
And when I'm down on my knees You pick me up
and bring me back to where You're my Rock.

One Body, One Spirit

1. Father we come to You in spirit and truth
    with our heart and our mind.
Father we come to You in spirit and truth
    with our heart and our mind.

Chorus
    One body, one spirit, one hope of our call.
    One faith and one baptism, one Father of all,
    Who is above all, and through all, and in us all.

2. Father I want to keep the unity
    of the spirit in the bond of peace.
Father I want to keep the unity
    of the spirit in the bond of peace.

Chorus 2
    One body, one spirit, one hope of our call.
    One faith and one baptism, one Father of all,
    One body, one spirit, one hope of our call.
    One faith and one baptism, one Father of all,
    Who is above all, and through all, and in us all.
    Who is above all, and through all, and in us all.

Bridge
    O Lord, let forgiveness rain down,
    let Your unity resound in our hearts.
    O Lord, let us learn to forgive,
    let Your children learn to live as one body.

Hold Me Now

Verse
O Lord, I need You now,
a shoulder to cry on,
that knows who I am,
To feel Your embrace, my Father,
to feel the warmth
of the light of Your face.

Chorus
Hold me, hold me now.
Whisper in my ear.
Remind me of who I am.
Speak Your love to my fears.
Hold me now.

The Lamb Who Was Slain

1. You have opened the door
   of the riches of God
And poured out Your life for the lost,
   the Lamb who was slain.
You erased all our sin,
   purchased men with Your blood
And made us as priests unto God,
   the Lamb who was slain.

Chorus
   You are worthy, You are faithful,
   You are holy, the Lamb who was slain.
   You are worthy, You are faithful,
   You are holy, the Lamb who was slain.

2. You came down as a man
   and You suffered the cross.
The King of the heavens became
   the Lamb who was slain.
But our God raised You up
   and our tongues now confess
That You are the Lord and the Christ,
   the Lamb who was slain.

See How Mercy

1. See how mercy's come to us,
   Sinners who deserve the cross.
   In our darkness and our shame,
   It's a wonder that He came.

2. See how grace has found a home
   In prodigals who love to roam.
   Such am I and such are we,
   Yet Father waits expectantly.

3. See how love's been redefined,
   Lives exchanged, His for mine.
   When on the cross He took my place,
   No doubt my Savior saw my face.

4. I long to say that I love You,
   A song alone will not do.
   The way I live my life each day,
   Let it be my gift of praise.

5. See how mercy's come to us,
   Sinners who deserve the cross.
   In our darkness and our shame,
   It's a wonder that He came.

CCLI Song #2976684

All of My Life

1. I have been through this before,
   Purify my heart again.
   When I am dry, You give me more.
   When I am full, You still give me more.
   I'm filled with You and I want more.

Chorus
   All of my life is in Your hands,
   All of my heart desires Your plans.
   Hold me here until this life is taken from me.
   O God, please draw me closer to You,
   Breathe on the things I say and do.
   Let my life chase only after You and glorify You.

2. With these words I come to You, Lord.
   Humbled servant, here I am.
   When I am dry, You give me more.
   When I am full, You still give me more.
   I'm filled with You and I want more.

We Fall Down

We fall down, we lay our crowns
  at the feet of Jesus.
The greatness of mercy and love
  at the feet of Jesus.

Chorus
  We cry, "Holy, holy, holy!"
  We cry, "Holy, holy, holy!"
  We cry, "Holy, holy, holy
    is the Lamb!"

Glory to You

Chorus

Glory to You, glory to You.
You are an awesome God!
Glory to You, glory to You.
You are an awesome God!

Verse

You are Father and Creator God,
Maker of heaven and Maker of Earth.
We worship You, we give You thanks.
We praise You!

Psalm 139
(Great Is Your Love)

Verse

Lord, You've searched me
and You know me,
when I sit, when I rise.
You understand my thoughts and my deeds
and I cannot hide from You.
Your thoughts toward me, O God,
outnumber all the sand.
And when I awake, I'm still with You,
held by Your hand.

Chorus

Great is Your love toward me,
Great is Your love toward me,
Great is Your love toward me, O God.

O Sacred King

Verse

 O sacred King, O holy King,
 How can I honor You rightly,
  honor that's fit for Your name?
 O sacred Friend, O holy Friend,
 I don't take what You give lightly,
  friendship instead of disgrace.

Chorus

 For it's the mystery of the universe,
  You're the God of holiness,
  Yet You welcome souls like me.
 And with the blessing of Your Father's heart
  You discipline the ones You love.
  There's kindness in Your majesty.
 Jesus, those who recognize Your power
  Know just how wonderful You are,
  that You draw near.

What a Friend I've Found

1. What a friend I've found,
   closer than a brother.
   I have felt Your touch,
   more intimate than lovers.

Chorus
   Jesus! Jesus!
   Jesus, friend forever!

2. What a hope I've found,
   more faithful than a mother.
   It would break my heart
   to ever lose each other.